EXPLORING
THEATER

Acting in
Theater

George Capaccio

Cavendish
Square
New York

Published in 2017 by Cavendish Square Publishing, LLC
243 5th Avenue, Suite 136, New York, NY 10016

Website: cavendishsq.com

This publication represents the opinions and views of the author based on his or her personal experience, knowledge, and research. The information in this book serves as a general guide only. The author and publisher have used their best efforts in preparing this book and disclaim liability rising directly or indirectly from the use and application of this book.

CPSIA Compliance Information: Batch #CW17CSQ

All websites were available and accurate when this book was sent to press.

Cataloging-in-Publication Data

Names: Capaccio, George.
Title: Acting in theater / George Capaccio.
Description: New York : Cavendish Square, 2017. | Series: Exploring theater | Includes index.
Identifiers: ISBN 9781502622693 (library bound) | ISBN 9781502622709 (ebook)
Subjects: LCSH: Acting--Juvenile literature. | Theater--Juvenile literature.
Classification: LCC PN2061.C36 2017 | DDC 792.02'8--dc23

The photographs in this book are used by permission and through the courtesy of: Cover Digital Vision/Photodisc/Getty Images; p. 4 Movie Poster Image Art/Getty Images; p. 7 Kyle Lee/Shutterstock.com; p. 10 Tinseltown/Shutterstock.com; p. 12 Lisa F. Young/Shutterstock.com; p. 13 Sergey Usovik/Shutterstock.com; p. 17 David M.Benett/Getty Images; p. 18 David M. Benett/Dave Benett/Getty Images; p. 21 Jim Spellman/WireImage; p. 24 Hill Street Studios/Blend Images/Getty Images; p. 26 SpeedKingz/Shutterstock. com; p. 30 Hill Street Studios/Blend Images/Getty Images; p. 33 Hill Street Studios/Blend Images/Getty Images; p. 35 Gregory Costanzo/Stone/Getty Images; p. 38 Joerg Koch/Getty Images Entertainment; p. 40 Hill Street Studios/Blend Images/Getty Images; p. 41 Catalin/Shutterstock.com; p. 44 RICHARD A.BROOKS/AFP/Getty Images; p. 47 AF archive/Alamy Stock Photo; p. 48 Dougal Waters/DigitalVision/Getty Images; p. 54 newzad/iStock/Thinkstock.com; p. 59 Hill Street Studios/Blend Images/Getty Images; p. 60 Mike Coppola/Getty Images; p. 64 Peter Bischoff/Getty Images; p. 67 Chesnot/Getty Images; p. 69 Leonard Mc Lane/DigitalVision/Getty Images; p. 70 Digital Vision/Photodisc/Thinkstock.com; p. 74 Hero Images/Getty Images; p. 78 Rawpixel.com/Shutterstock.com; p. 82 Olimpik/Shutterstock.com; p. 85 Sylvain Gaboury/FilmMagic/Getty Images; p. 86 Sergiy Palamarchuk/Shutterstock.com.

Printed in the United States of America

CONTENTS

Robert De Niro worked as a cabbie for weeks to prepare for his role in *Taxi Driver*.

CHAPTER ONE

AN ACTOR'S TOOLBOX

When Robert De Niro, a famous Hollywood actor, lands a role in a new film, he doesn't just learn his lines and show up for rehearsals. He prepares for the part by doing whatever he can to experience the life his character has lived. In the movie *Taxi Driver*, for example, De Niro played Travis Bickle, a troubled combat veteran who makes a living driving a cab in the 1970s in New York City. The movie showcased De Niro's remarkable ability to create believable characters. To prepare for this role, he lost 35 pounds (16 kilograms), obtained a cab driver's license, and worked as a cab driver for several weeks in New York.

In response to an interviewer's questions about how he prepares for acting roles, he said, "Actors must expose themselves to the surroundings and keep their minds obsessed with that … You've got to physically and mentally become that person you are portraying."

Of course, acting students in school or community theater programs are not expected to prepare for a role the way Robert De Niro and other professional actors do. Nevertheless, every role, whether for film or theater, requires preparation, and the whole purpose of this preparation is to make the character you're playing as real and believable as possible—not just to the audience but to you, the actor.

Have you ever thought about acting on the stage? If so, have you wondered what you need to do in order to become really good at it? Or maybe you've thought that acting is easy; anybody can do it. Like first-rate athletes, good actors can make what they do look effortless. But in fact, they've mastered their craft so thoroughly you don't see all the work that went into perfecting their performance. An effective onstage performance is the fruit of many hours of work, and this work has to do with practicing and refining the necessary skills—but always with one goal in mind: to develop a character that is true to the playwright's intentions and serves the overall direction, or point of view, of the play.

An actor's "toolbox" of skills involves much more than learning lines and knowing where and when to move on stage. The most basic acting skills include the following:

- Self-awareness

- Verbal and physical mastery

- Understanding the script

- Discipline and teamwork

Self-Awareness

Foremost among these skills is self-awareness. If beginning actors don't know themselves very well and aren't in touch with their own needs and

Actors can draw on disappointments, such as athletic failures, while on stage.

feelings, it will be difficult for them to identify with a character's needs and feelings and the purposes behind that character's behavior. Self-awareness is very important no matter what stage of development an actor has reached. And as people become more aware of the different sides of their personality, the more fully they are able to enter the life of a character who might at first seem too unfamiliar.

Suppose you have been cast as someone who is awkward in social situations, doesn't have many friends, and has a hard time expressing feelings. If you are outgoing, very sociable, and have an extroverted personality, you might decide you can't possibly play the part you've been given. However, if you do your "homework" by examining your life more closely, you might recall a time or a situation when you felt somewhat like your character.

For example, maybe you tried out for one of your school's athletic teams. Suppose some of the other students at the tryout were exceptional athletes, and their prowess on the field made you doubt your abilities. When it was your turn to show the coach what you could do, maybe you lost your confidence and didn't perform as well as you could have. You could use this or similar personal experiences to help you identify with the character you're playing and bring the character's inner world to life in your performance.

Verbal and Physical Mastery

Like athletes, actors have to be in good shape or they won't be able to perform well on stage. While athletes get in shape through strenuous exercise—like running, lifting weights, or using cardio machines—actors focus on making their voice and body as expressive and supple as possible. Acting, like playing a sport, is a physical activity that can be exhausting, especially if the actor has not gotten into the condition needed to handle the demands of a live performance.

Of course, physical exercise benefits both the actor and the athlete by developing strength and endurance. But actors also have to acquire vocal mastery. One aspect of vocal mastery for actors is **projection**—the ability to use their voices effectively, without straining or injuring their vocal cords. Unless a theater has excellent **acoustics** or the actors are wearing microphones, they have to deliver their lines loudly enough to reach audience members who are farthest from the stage.

In addition to projection, actors also need to develop vocal flexibility and expressiveness in order to convincingly convey a character's particular accent or speech patterns, and whatever emotions are required. Think of Johnny Depp's performance as Captain Jack Sparrow in *Pirates of the Caribbean*. If you've seen the movie, then you may remember how his character had a very unique way of speaking and moving. Depp revealed that he "borrowed"

Johnny Depp modeled his character Jack Sparrow after guitar player Keith Richards.

the speech patterns and physical mannerisms of Rolling Stones guitarist Keith Richards to create the character of Jack Sparrow.

Becoming adept at using your voice to express your character's feelings and particular way of speaking also requires good **diction** and breath control. These skills, when practiced and honed, will help you achieve vocal mastery. The words and phrases we use to express our thoughts and feelings—and the way we say them out loud—are what constitute our diction. In a play, the playwright has already decided how each character speaks. The choice of words reflects how the writer envisions the characters. As an actor, one of your major responsibilities is to bring these words to life, to make them come across to the audience as exactly right for each moment of the play or each scene in which your character appears.

Our voice tells others a great deal about who we are, our personality. In fact, the word "personality" derives from the ancient Greek word for "mask" and the translation of *per sona*, "through sound." In your development as an actor, you will eventually discover how you can use your voice to express your character. But to do this, you will need to turn your voice into a flexible, responsive instrument capable of conveying a range of emotions.

In theater, effective vocal projection is not limited to speaking loudly enough for others to hear what you're saying; more importantly, it's about **articulation**—speaking clearly, so that others not only hear but understand what you're saying. Actors can improve their ability to articulate—that is, to pronounce words clearly and accurately—by understanding how spoken language is produced: what muscles and other parts of the body are involved in turning breath into speech.

There are numerous exercises that help actors improve the quality of their voices and their ability to project and creatively adjust tone, pitch, and tempo (how fast or slow the character speaks). The ultimate aim of these exercises is breath control. A trained actor understands and uses the natural unity

Vocal training teaches you how using different chambers of your body can change the quality of your voice.

of breath, voice, emotion, and movement to express character or, in other words, to breathe life into the person being portrayed.

In addition to vocal mastery, an actor needs to acquire physical mastery. Just as training and exercises will help transform the voice into a flexible and expressive instrument, proper training will do the same for the actor's body. Many theater programs emphasize fencing, gymnastics, and dancing as activities that will develop strength, coordination, flexibility, and responsiveness. These essential qualities enable the actor to "embody" the character in specific gestures and movements.

In stage combat, actors learn how to express their characters through the conflict.

Every person, or character, has a particular way of moving. Have you ever picked out someone you know in a crowd without seeing their face or even hearing their voice? Maybe it was the way they held their shoulders or tilted their head or swung their arms while walking. You identified the person at once from the smallest detail of their particular way of moving. As an actor explores a character, he or she might experiment with different ways of moving until finding one that really feels right. A young, free-spirited character will not move the same way as an older, world-weary character. Similarly, someone who lives in their own mind much of the time will move quite differently from someone who is more open hearted or heart centered. Student actors can experiment with moving from different centers of the body—head, heart, gut, or groin. Each center, when used as a point of focus by the actor, will yield ways of moving unique to that center.

But an actor's physical preparation doesn't stop with the exploration of moving from different centers of the body. The purpose of this and other forms of physical preparation is to create a believable character with their own unique way of doing things, from walking in or out of a room to picking up a cup, taking a coat from a guest, or handling a priceless object.

Understanding the Script

Text analysis is another key aspect of an actor's training. In practice, this means being able to read

Guys and Dolls requires a
unified effort from a very large
ensemble to succeed.

deeply into the play's script. An actor needs to understand what makes a character "tick," or in other words, what motivates them, what do they want—in the play as a whole and in each scene. However, the actor also needs to know how the character relates to the other characters in the play and why they relate that way. Text analysis doesn't stop there.

Beyond this basic understanding of the script, it's important for actors to study the time and place of the play. Is the play set in a contemporary location, like a neighborhood in New York City, or someplace in the past, like Venice in the sixteenth century? Whatever the play's setting, the actor's job is to do a certain amount of background research so that his or her performance is true to where and when the play takes place.

Compare the setting of *Ruined*, a play by Lynn Nottage, with *Spike Heels* by Theresa Rebeck. In *Ruined*, a businesswoman named Mama Nadi runs a bar in the Democratic Republic of the Congo during that country's brutal civil war. She employs young women who have been severely hurt by the war and protects them from the world outside. By contrast, *Spike Heels* is a comedy. The setting is Boston in the present, where the characters explore what it means to be a woman in today's world and how men are (or are not) adapting to the influence of **feminism**. Actors performing in either play have their work cut out for them; they need to understand how the setting, which includes time and place as well as significant social or cultural developments, affects the characters and their interactions.

Discipline and Teamwork

All of the acting skills discussed so far have little benefit without discipline, which is its own kind of skill. Discipline means working on the technical, or craft, elements of acting with as much regularity as you can build into your schedule. It means showing up on time for rehearsals, learning your lines in a timely manner, and respecting the director, fellow actors, the stage manager, and members of the technical crew. These include the lighting, sound, and set designers, and the prop master/mistress. Discipline also means respecting yourself and what you can contribute to the overall experience of producing a play. An actor is part of a team, and putting on a play is a team effort. While actors are not all equally talented or skilled, they are all equally responsible for the final result—the quality of the performance in front of an audience.

Elton John (in sunglasses) created the music for *Billy Elliot the Musical*.

CHAPTER TWO
CREATING AN ENSEMBLE

Putting on a play is a team effort, and everyone on the team has a job to do. Even outstanding actors who really shine onstage and might be described as the stars of the show wouldn't shine so brightly without the hard work and support of everyone else involved in the production. The entire cast of the play *God of Carnage* received Tony nominations for lead actor/actress. Since there were only four actors in the play, nominating all four was an exceptional turn of events in modern theater. (The play is about two couples whose sons have gotten into a playground scuffle. The parents meet in order to figure out how to deal with the boys. Their attempt to have a polite, civilized discussion eventually breaks down as the more aggressive sides of their personalities begin to emerge.) After the cast was nominated, Jeff Daniels, one of the actors, said, "When it comes to success in acting, people often think of the sole actor, the 'I'm ready for my close-up' sense of me, me, me," he said. "But in our play and others this season, the interdependence of the actors is key."

The play *Billy Elliot the Musical* tells the story of a boy in a mining town in the North of England. The play is based on the movie *Billy Elliot*, which came out in 2000. In both cases, Billy discovers his talent for dancing and aspires to learn ballet, something his father, a coal miner, can't accept. In the Broadway production, three young actors took turns playing the part of Billy Elliot. Instead of becoming rivals, the boys became close friends who attributed their success to the support they gave each other. After all three were jointly awarded a best actor prize, Kiril Kulish, one of the winners, said, "Playing Billy would be impossible for me if there weren't the other Billys."

His fellow actor Trent Kowalik agreed: "We don't actually see each other that much now, because we have different performances. But we learned from each other's strengths in rehearsals. And it's really good to get and give moral support to each other." Giving and receiving moral support is an important part of teamwork, without which the challenging work of putting on a play would have less chance of succeeding.

In another musical—*West Side Story*—two rival teenage gangs, the Sharks and the Jets, compete for dominance in New York City. The members of the Jets, led by Tony, are all white; the Sharks, led by Bernardo, are Puerto Rican. Karen Olivo, the actress who played Anita, Bernardo's sister, in a 2009 Broadway production, credited the success of her performance with the support she received from the other girls in the gang. "They're like my little sisters," she said. "Several of them haven't done a whole lot of shows before. They sometimes ask me,

Karen Olivo (*center*) credited her success in *West Side Story* to her "sisters" in the cast.

'How do we fill out this form?' or 'What do we do here?'"

Sometimes directors will go to great lengths to get the kind of rapport they're looking for among their actors. For example, Richard Linklater, writer-director of the 2016 movie *Everybody Wants Some!!*, wanted his actors to experience a close, brotherly feeling toward each other. In the movie, they play college baseball teammates who get together during the weekend before the new semester begins. To achieve the feeling he was going after, he "required the actors to live together for two and a half weeks before rehearsals started. They established relationships while staying in a cabin on his Texas ranch, which carried over to present-day."

Sharing a Texas ranch wasn't the only requirement the actors had to meet before filming began; they also had to play baseball, like a real team, during the actual rehearsal period.

Directors and drama teachers can employ a range of games and exercises to help build teamwork and foster a collaborative spirit among the students and/or actors. Lorraine Thompson is an actress and the head of the Drama Department at Athens Academy in Georgia. She believes strongly in getting her acting students to work together as a team. And her efforts are paying off. One of the judges who evaluated her students' work during the performances of one-act plays made the following comment after the competition: "I want to start by saying that I have never seen such amazing **ensemble** work! I was watching so much more than a play about a town. I was watching a [real] town. Well done!"

Thompson's students were thrilled. "High fives and hugs rippled throughout the room. As far as they were concerned, they had already received the highest praise they could. They had reached their goal of [creating an] ensemble."

In theater, an ensemble is not the same as a cast of players. In an ensemble, the actors are still part of a team striving toward the same goal, but they are also working more closely with the director to generate ideas for staging, character development, and the overall shape of the play. Moreover, in an ensemble, there is no star. Every performer, whatever their role happens to be, is expected to work at their highest level. Sanford Robbins, head of the University of Delaware's theater department, compares ensemble work to sports: "It's rare that an all-star team is as good as a really good regular team, even though you may pick the best players. In ensemble acting, there's a cohesion and harmony in the way the roles are played … and the sum is more powerful than the parts."

Creating an ensemble is not easy. It takes teamwork, commitment to the process, and discipline. It's one thing to tell actors "There are no small parts, only small players," or "You're all equal parts of one whole." But to make this a reality, cast members must be willing to work together and encourage each other to do their best. Otherwise, there's a risk that conflict, frustration, and tension may result, and these things can slow down the work and compromise the quality of the production. Putting a show together can be an immensely rewarding experience for everyone involved. It can also be stressful, especially if cast members don't get along or if their personal schedules conflict with the production schedule. Maybe some of the actors in a student production, for example, have competing demands on their time and have to miss rehearsals. Technical problems can also cause stress and strain and consequently gnaw away at the spirit of teamwork. Suppose the set designers are working behind schedule; opening night is coming, and the

In ensemble theater, the director gives the actors more freedom to experiment.

main set pieces are still under construction. The actors need to rehearse with a completed set. The director is frustrated because only part of the set is available, and those frustrations affect the actors, who start griping about one thing or another.

Another example of a stressful situation that can impact teamwork is the presence of one or more **prima donnas** in the cast. These are actors who view themselves as indispensable and believe their talent is far superior to anyone else's. For them, the play is mainly a vehicle to showcase their star power to an adoring audience. Such individuals may find it difficult to work as part of a team and to share the spotlight with their fellow actors.

Of course, in any theatrical production, actors are not only working with other actors; they are also interacting with members of the technical crew, the director, the stage manager(s), and whoever is in charge of publicity. All of these relationships require a willingness to treat others with respect and to see them as partners in the creation of a theatrical experience. In some respects, a successful play is like a smoothly running machine in which all the parts are meshing with each other without undue friction. The players make up one of the parts. They can't do their job without the support they receive from the people responsible for sound and lighting, set design, and costumes and makeup.

At various points in the rehearsal process, actors will need to meet with the costumer to have measurements taken for whatever outfits they will be wearing in the play. The person in charge of sound

A night of karaoke is an effective way for the cast to build team spirit.

will need to adjust sound levels for actors wearing microphones. In plays with specific sound effects, the actors will need to anticipate sound cues and adjust the timing of their lines accordingly. If the script calls for a train whistle at a particular moment in the play, actors onstage may need to pause briefly so the sound of the whistle is audible and not muffled by the dialogue.

Some productions use highly complex lighting cues (and sound cues too!) that are programmed in a computer. Even with less complex lighting directions, actors will need to know where the light is coming from onstage and where they need to be in order to be properly illuminated. For example, a production of William Shakespeare's romantic tragedy *Romeo and Juliet* may require Juliet to appear in a soft blue light during a **soliloquy**. The actress playing Juliet had better know where she's supposed to stand when the blue accent light appears. If she doesn't, then the audience may hear her words but have a hard time seeing her.

Team-Building Activities for Actors

Ideally, team building is about creating a community of individuals, each of whom feels empowered to work at his or her highest level. In the process of becoming a community, cast members will learn to support their fellow performers, improve their ability to communicate effectively, become better listeners, and express empathy when appropriate. Here are some ways of building a community.

1. Character Background

Each actor completes a worksheet that provides details about the character he or she is playing. The worksheet could include such elements as name, age, daily routine, relationships with other characters, and major goal(s). During the rehearsal period, actors can share the information on their worksheets; this way, the entire cast has a clearer picture of each other's characters.

2. Getting to Know You (sort of like "speed dating")

Actors form two groups of equal size—A and B. Each group sits in a line directly opposite the other group. Each pair of opposing actors has one minute to share something about the characters they're playing. When time is called, group B moves down one place. The person at the end of the group B line moves to the beginning of the line and introduces himself or herself to the person at the start of group A. The sharing continues until all actors in both groups have had a chance to introduce their character.

3. All Hands on Deck!

In this team-building activity, the entire cast works together to complete a project or participate in an activity, preferably one connected with some aspect of the play. Suppose a group of middle school students is putting on a play about Victor Frankenstein, the obsessed scientist who dreams of creating life and succeeds in creating a monster. To build team spirit, the director might provide a collection of found objects and let the actors work together to assemble the objects into a large, puppet-like character or creature that suggests Frankenstein's monster.

Emma!, a musical comedy by Eric Price, concerns a matchmaking high school senior (Emma) who hopes to find a boyfriend for her shy sophomore friend, Harriet. The play features a selection of tunes from 1960s girl groups and contemporary solo performers like Katy Perry and Avril Lavigne. For a group project, cast members could take part in an informal "sing-a-long" of popular tunes.

For the production of *Quilters*, a musical about a mother and six other women (called her daughters) living during the pioneer era of American history, the director gave the actors pieces of fabric from the costumes they would wear in the show. They sewed the pieces together to make a quilt, which was put on sale in the theater lobby. At the end of the run, the cast presented the quilt to the director in recognition of all she had given to them.

Reading aloud from a script without any preparation is called a cold reading.

CHAPTER THREE

THREE STEPS OF PRODUCTION

When you go to a theater to watch a play, you're seeing the final result of months of preparation on the part of everyone involved: actors, director, stage manager, technical crew, and publicists, among other participants. This preparatory work and the actual performances make up the production process, which happens in three distinct steps or stages: preproduction, rehearsal, and performance.

Preproduction

If your school or local community theater is producing a play, and you want to be one of the actors, the first step is being cast. Typically, a casting notice will appear on your school or your town's website announcing a time and place when auditions will be held. Notices might also go up on information boards around the school or in places around town where people are likely to see them. They might also appear in the local school newsletter or town newspaper.

Professional actors (actors who pursue acting as a career) may hire a talent agent—or artist's manager—whose job is to find work for the actors he or she represents. If an agent spots a role in an upcoming theatrical production that seems right for one of his or her actors, the agent will submit that actor's **headshot** and résumé to the play's casting director. The casting director, in turn, will invite potential candidates to an audition.

Auditions

The beginning or student actor, like the professional, still has to pass an audition. Auditions can be stressful experiences, especially if the student isn't prepared. One of the best ways of preparing is to be sure you know what the play is about. Read it thoroughly beforehand.

It isn't always possible to know in advance what part you will be asked to audition for. However, it can't hurt to determine beforehand which role or roles you most closely identify with. That way, if the casting director asks you to read for one of those parts, you're already ahead of the game.

Setting aside time to do some relaxation and warm-up exercises before the audition will boost your energy level and get you ready to give the audition your best shot. Slow, deep breathing is an effective way to relax and focus, and warming up can be as simple as doing a five-minute workout or a short run. If you know tai chi or other martial arts forms, performing a few moves can also reduce stress and any anxiety you might feel about the upcoming audition.

There are different types of auditions depending on the type of play being produced, the artistic

Study the script for clues you can use before auditioning for a specific character.

preferences of the director, the type of setting in which it will be performed, and the audience for which it is intended. For a musical like *West Side Story*, the director will be looking for performers who can act, dance, and sing, and may utilize a choreographer and music coach to manage parts of the audition. For non-musical dramas and comedies, you will most likely be asked to read all or part of a character's **monologue** or to read a scene with other actors. Prepare your own monologue, one that shows your strengths, in case you are asked to perform one. It should last about one minute. The director wants to see how well you understand what your character is doing in the scene and how clearly you communicate your character's thoughts and feelings.

Creating a Backstory

The actor who succeeds in getting cast in a play can start working on his or her part even before rehearsals begin. The work will depend on the nature of the role and the type of play. In the beginning of my own acting career, I was cast as Sir Anthony Absolute in a British comedy called *The Rivals*. Like his name implies, Sir Anthony sees life in absolute terms. Things are right or wrong, black or white. There are no shades of gray. He has already decided whom his son will marry, and if the young man refuses, Sir Anthony will cut him out of his will.

The setting of the play is London in the late 1700s. The characters are mostly members of the British upper class. Once I knew I would be playing the part of Sir Anthony Absolute, I started reading

Knowing the details of style
and society can prepare you for
a period piece.

about life in eighteenth-century London and how people with power and wealth like Sir Anthony would have dressed and behaved. From my reading, I learned that upper-class men wore expensive shoes with high, red heels to show the world they would never stoop to working with their hands. So I went to a thrift shop and bought an old pair of men's shoes with unusually high heels, which I painted bright red. I wore the shoes during the run of the show, along with a wig and other costume pieces appropriate for eighteenth-century gentlemen.

In my research, I also learned about the English **Restoration**—the historical period in which the play was written—and the styles of speaking, moving, and acting in Restoration-era comedies like *The Rivals*.

Jean Schiffman, an arts journalist, wrote a column for the online blog *Backstage* in which she noted the influence of fashion during the eighteenth century on the way actors moved onstage: "It goes without saying that a bustle, a corset, and an elaborate headdress necessitate different movement than do your everyday jeans and flip-flops. For men it's the same thing: High-heeled shoes, tight trousers, decorative swords dangling from your waist, and heavy wigs dictate part of your physicality."

The way people move, Schiffman observes, is an expression of the times in which they live and their place in society. The same true is for the way they speak. Language in Restoration comedies poses a serious challenge to modern actors, who have to "deliver this language elegantly, playfully."

Once I was familiar with the historical period and the main features of Restoration theater, I was ready to take another step in my preproduction work: developing my character—Sir Anthony Absolute. I wanted to build a foundation for what he says and does during the time span of the play. The script says very little about Sir Anthony's life before the action of the play begins. So, using the knowledge I had gained from my reading and a bit of imagination, I invented what today might be called my character's "**backstory**"—how he spent his childhood and early adulthood, what his marriage was like, how he became such an influential member of society, etc.

Finding Things in Common

Another important part of preproduction work for an aspiring actor is making **substitutions**. To make the character as real as possible for both actor and audience, actors can substitute actual material from their own lives for the events and circumstances their character confronts. What he or she experiences during the play and what you have personally lived through may be very different. So what do you do in order to connect with this stranger you're eventually going to portray onstage before an audience?

The answer is to look for any similarities between your life and that of your character. If you search for a literal, one-to-one correspondence, you're going to be disappointed unless your life and your character's perfectly match, which rarely happens. So you need to look below the surface of your particular life experiences for something that is probably true for a lot of people, including the character you're playing.

Suppose you've been cast in a community theater production of the musical *West Side Story*, and you're playing the part of Tony, a former member of the Jets, one of the two gangs in the musical. Tony meets Maria at a dance, and the two fall in love. The problem is that Maria is the sister of Bernardo, the leader of the rival gang—the Sharks. In real life, you've never been part of a gang, you don't live in New York City (the setting of the musical), and your girlfriend is not from a rival gang.

Your experiences could prepare you to play Tony or Maria in *West Side Story*.

In your hunt for substitutions, you might explore what it was like to join one of your school's athletic teams or to have close ties with a small group of friends at school or in the neighborhood. You could use the feelings you associate with these experiences to make your onstage membership in a street gang start to feel real for you. You don't have to live in New York City to know something about what it's like to live in a large metropolis. Even if you live in a quiet suburb or a small town, there are plenty of movies and TV shows that depict life in New York and other big cities. (Even lousy movies and shows are useful resources if the setting or the situation mirrors elements in the play.) You could watch some of them to get a sense of what it would be like to grow up in a tough neighborhood and to join a gang for protection as well as camaraderie.

As for the romance that develops between Tony and Maria in *West Side Story*, you might focus on how risky, even dangerous, their relationship is. Tony is white; Maria is Puerto Rican. According to the mindset of their respective friends and families, they should never have gotten romantically involved or even become friends.

But no matter how different Tony and Maria's ethnic backgrounds are, they are dealing with a common, universal problem: prejudice against someone who is perceived by others as different and therefore unacceptable. This is where the actor's work of making substitutions can help him connect emotionally with the difficulties Tony and Maria are facing. Have you ever had to overcome prejudice in your life or stood up for something you believed in, even at the risk of alienating your friends? For that matter, have you ever become friends with someone from a background entirely different from your own?

These are the sorts of questions that enable actors to get below the literal meaning of their

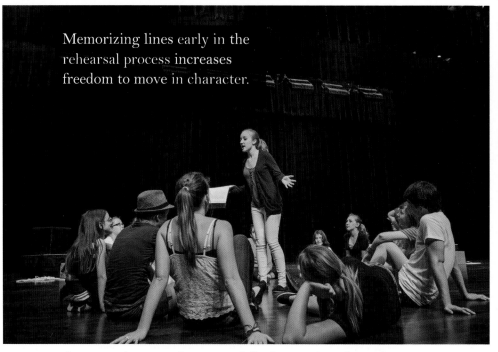

Memorizing lines early in the rehearsal process increases freedom to move in character.

character's experience and find emotional truths that will serve them in the play. Keep in mind that the background research and character development that begin during preproduction are building the foundation of what comes later in the process— rehearsals and performances.

Rehearsals

During the initial rehearsal, actors will likely read through the entire play with minimal feedback from the director. What happens during this first rehearsal is a bit like going out on a first date with someone. You might have already formed a pretty good idea about the person you're taking out, but once you're in each other's company, who knows what you'll discover. Your date might possess hidden virtues or annoying habits you never dreamed about. Or maybe the way that person treats other people makes you wonder why in the world you're so interested in them.

As actors read their lines aloud with fellow actors, they need to pay close attention to their immediate reactions to what their character does and says and how that character interacts with the others. These reactions are like the first impressions we receive when we meet someone new. It may turn out later they are completely "off the mark," and so we need to revise our understanding of someone. On the other hand, our first impressions may prove to be very keen insights into someone's personality. The same holds true for actors reading their parts for the first time. The experience will give them sudden glimpses into their characters' private, inner worlds; hints about what makes them do what they do in the play (motivations) and what keeps them from getting what they want (**obstacles**).

Make journal entries detailing what you learned about your character after each rehearsal.

Some actors find it useful to keep track of the images, ideas, insights, and feelings that occur to them during a read-through with the entire cast. They might make notes in the margins of the script, or underline or highlight key lines or passages.

Another option for actors is to keep a paper or electronic journal in which to record their thoughts about the play and the character. This record keeping is not required, but it does serve as a useful tool in the rehearsal process.

The information that comes from this first encounter with the role makes up another set of building blocks the actor can use in shaping a character. However, if an actor goes into the rehearsal process with strong, preconceived ideas about the character, he is likely to cut short his own creative process and never succeed in creating something original and believable.

Keeping a Journal

The job of an actor is to make a character come across as an individual with their own way of looking, speaking, moving, gesturing, and just being. Ideally, this individuality should enliven not only the big moments in the play when emotions are running high, but the details as well. This includes even the smallest of details, such as how a character enters and exits a room, or drinks a glass of water. Here's where a journal will come in handy. It doesn't matter if the journal is a spiral notebook, a loose-leaf binder, or a file on your computer. What does matter is having a place where you can store your thoughts and observations about the play and the character you're playing. In the journal, you can continue the work you began when you were doing your background research. However, now you're adding more specific details about your character—not just inventing a biography—beginning with physical facts: Is he old or young, tall or short, muscular or overweight? How does he dress? Does he walk with a swagger in his step, or does he take small, tentative steps as if he were afraid of his own shadow?

From these basic facts, you can delve more deeply into what sort of person you're playing. Your imagination, observations of the people around you, and clues provided in the script are all you need to take this next step in developing your character. In your journal, you might list your character's favorite foods and hobbies. Does the person live alone or as part of a large family? What does this person like to do when alone? Does he or she have a lot of friends, or is the character more of a loner? How are setbacks and disappointments handled? Does the person get angry and curse, or is he or she likely to stay calm?

Of course, you won't necessarily find answers to such questions in the script. They are only intended to get you thinking more deeply about your character. As you continue your exploration, you will need to make choices about the kind of person your character is. These choices are what will make the character stand out as a one-of-a-kind individual. The backstory you may have created during the preproduction stage will contribute to your character development; as you get more involved in the rehearsals, you might have to revise this story by adding details or changing first impressions as your understanding increases.

Give yourself time to wonder about your character's inner life instead of only focusing on personal history or the outer details of their life, like taste in music or clothing. What are their hopes and dreams? What do they want to become? Are they happy with the choices they have made in life? What if they won $1 million? How would they spend the money? If they were a type of building, a movie star, or an automobile, which one would they be? Animals are a great source of ideas for actors in the process of creating a character. The way animals move, the sounds they make, their behavior, and how they express their emotions can inspire actors to incorporate some of these qualities into their characters. Other people are another great source of ideas. You might spot someone on the street who strikes you as similar to how you imagine your character. Get out your journal and jot down some details about that person's appearance and way of moving. Better yet, add a simple sketch to your notes to make the person that much easier to recall.

Your Character's Journey

So rehearsals are under way in earnest. The director is beginning to work on individual scenes. Each scene has its own rhythm, its own shape, and its own role to play in the overall direction of the play. As the actor works on her scenes in rehearsal, she'll develop a keener sense of her character's path from the beginning to the end of the play. Another name for this path is "**arc**." Each part of a play—the different acts and the scenes within each act—has its own arc, or trajectory. The same is true for the life of each character. A character's arc is the changes he or she undergoes in the course of the play. This is certainly the case for the main characters and may also be true for the minor characters. If you are playing one of the major characters, you need to determine what these changes are, and what or who is driving them.

In William Shakespeare's play *Macbeth* (also called *The Scottish Play*), a Scottish noblewoman—Lady Macbeth—plots with her husband to murder King Duncan. The king has come to visit them in their castle. Lady Macbeth wants her husband to become the new king and is positive this is also what he wants. In the beginning of the play, she is determined to see to it that Duncan never leaves the castle alive. Her scheming makes her seem ruthless, but in fact she has a strong conscience, which she attempts to keep under wraps. Macbeth, her husband, commits the murder. But his wife's remorse and sense of guilt finally get the better of her. By the end of the play, she is so tormented by guilt that she kills herself. Lady Macbeth has gone from being an ambitious woman in pursuit of power to a guilt-ridden, suicidal figure. That is one way to think about the arc of her journey.

Exploring Your Character's Needs and Objectives

Rehearsals are when actors get to explore their characters, and this involves a certain amount of experimenting. Rarely do actors begin the rehearsal process with a complete understanding of the

SECRET OF SUCCESS

In 2015, Viola Davis became the first African American woman to win an Emmy for Outstanding Lead Actress in a Drama Series—*How to Get Away with Murder*. A few years earlier, Davis received Academy Award nominations for Best Actress in *The Help* and for Best Supporting Actress for her performance in the film version of *Doubt*, which also featured Philip Seymour Hoffman. In addition to her television and film credits, Davis has also won critical acclaim for her strong performances in Broadway shows.

Davis was born on her grandmother's farm in South Carolina but grew up in Rhode Island. Her father groomed horses at local racetracks, and her mother worked as a maid while also participating in the struggle for civil rights. Davis found an escape from her family's financial struggles by watching movies in local cinemas. "We grew up in abject poverty. Acting, writing scripts and skits were a way of escaping our environment at a very young age," she said. As a result of performing in high school plays, she realized how much she loved acting. After graduation, she attended Rhode Island College and majored in theater, getting her degree in 1988. From there, Davis enrolled in the Juilliard School for performing arts in New York City.

It wasn't long before she started attracting attention while acting in various New York theaters. In 1996, Davis appeared in her first Broadway production. Around the same time, she began landing roles in TV series and films while continuing to perform on New York stages. In 2011, Davis starred in *The Help*, in which she played a maid in Mississippi during the civil rights era of the early 1960s.

She was familiar with the life of a maid from watching her mother. She shared other details of how she prepared to play Aibileen Clark in *The Help* in an interview with *The Collider* published on August 9, 2011.

Viola Davis showed her versatility in the acclaimed film *The Help*.

"One of the things that I wanted to create, even in the hair, was that every small detail was to show what she does to put on that wig every day. Black women wear wigs, and we wore wigs then. That's just what we do. We have a hair issue. But, I wanted to do it subtly. You have the image of her in the bathtub with her cornrows, and then she has her wig on in the next shot. That's what she does before she goes to work. She puts her wig on. How she looks when she is in a room full of white women is very important to her. I thought about all the details, even in the way she dresses when she goes to work and the way she reacts when Skeeter [a white women writing about the lives of African American maids in the South] comes in the house. That was very difficult for Aibileen. She's never had a white person in the house, so she's serving her. All of that comes from doing your work, as an actress. Your job is to make it authentic and make it connected to something very human. It's what you have to do."

Macbeth and Lady Macbeth,
reveal their innermost
thoughts and motives.

part they're playing. During rehearsals, they get to try out their ideas and discover which ones are workable and which ones need to be discarded. They also get to refine and deepen their understanding of their character by playing different **objectives**, or intentions. A character's objective is what he or she wants to achieve in a particular scene. The playwright doesn't necessarily spell out his characters' objectives, though in some plays, the objectives are fairly straightforward. They're not hidden in the script, waiting for the actors to discover them. Two actresses playing Lady Macbeth in Shakespeare's play will likely come up with their own interpretations of the character and her objectives, and these differences will show up in how they perform the part.

We all have objectives that affect what we do and the choices we make. The same is true in theater. Actors have to identify their characters' objectives. During rehearsals, they can try out different ones to see which ones have the greatest amount of energy behind them. Some objectives fall flat. They don't fully engage the actor. He might decide that in scene A his character (who is sixteen years old) wants to prove to his parents that he can take care of himself and is old enough to quit school. But during rehearsal, the actor discovers that when he delivers his lines, they come out sounding flat and lifeless. They lack the energy of a strongly desired objective. So he experiments with different objectives until he finds one that really "clicks" and makes the scene come to life. For this to happen, an objective has to connect with something inside the actor. He has to "feel it."

When blocking scenes for a play, a director will show actors where to go and when.

After all, no matter what the role, an actor's main resource is himself—his life experiences, his feelings, thoughts, and memories, but translated into the life of his character. Getting back to our actor playing a sixteen-year-old who wants to leave school, a more successful objective, one that connects with the emotional core of the scene and of the character, might be to "make my parents see the unique individual I am and to stop treating me like a kid."

Behind every objective, there's a need. The goals we pursue in life stem from our needs, which include the need for approval and acceptance, for love and companionship, for physical well-being and a meaningful life. We may not always be aware of these needs in our lives, but when rehearsing a role in a play, it helps to get in touch with our character's needs. In the language of the theater, to "play an objective" is to let these needs energize the actor's actions and the way he or she relates to the other characters. Needs are like fuel. Getting in touch with them is like switching on a source of power.

Once again, your journal will come in handy as you experiment with different objectives and begin to identify your character's needs. Which objectives really pulled you into the scene? Which ones just didn't work? The journal is where you can keep track of what happened during rehearsals (and also during performances). It's a record of your character's development "from the page to the stage." And it's where you can write down your thoughts and reflections not only about your character but about the play and what it means to you, and about your relationships with the other characters.

Charting a Plan of Action

At some point during rehearsals, the director will begin **blocking** the scenes. Until this point, he or she will typically allow the actors to move freely in the performing space as they deliver their lines. When you watch a play, the characters are moving according to a plan that has been worked out carefully during rehearsals. Creating this plan is what it means to block a play, scene by scene. (These plans are a bit like the running plays used in football to move the ball down the field. In theater, the purpose of blocking is to move the action of the play in a well-orchestrated pattern.)

The actors are expected to take careful notes, so they can follow the blocking during subsequent rehearsals and later, during performances. Marking up the script with blocking notes is how many actors handle this phase of the work. Their notes might indicate, for instance, when to cross from stage right to stage left, or when to cross from upstage to downstage, or how long to stand by the table at center stage before making an exit.

Stage movement is always for a specific purpose. Ideally, it both serves the scene and supports an actor's motivation—the reason why they do what they do. Think about your own movements during a typical day. When you get home from school, you drop your book bag on the floor by the door and head for the kitchen. What's to eat? You open one of the cupboards and take down a favorite snack food. Then you find a plate, sit down at the table, and put the food on the plate. There's a pile of mail on the table. Better have a look. Who knows, there might be a letter of acceptance from one of the colleges you applied to. So you sort though the mail while gobbling your snack.

The movements you've just made are routine; you don't need to think too much about them. You do them unconsciously. But onstage, you have to be aware of how you move and why—your motivation for moving the way you do. When you sorted through the mail, you did it for a specific reason—to find the letter you've been waiting for. Similarly, when the director tells you to move from upstage left to downstage right, you need to know why. What does that cross have to do with what your character wants in this scene?

Blocking also takes into account sound and lighting cues, which actors must be aware of throughout the performance. Movement, sound, and lighting are parts of one theatrical reality. A well-blocked play will make sure actors are where they're supposed to be when specific sound and lighting effects happen. And the actors, of course, need to be sure they know the blocking so well that they don't need to think about it during the performance.

Learning Your Lines

When do actors do the grunt work of learning their lines? That depends on the actor and in some cases on the director. Some directors want actors to memorize their part early in the rehearsal period. Being "**off book**" gives actors more freedom of movement and more opportunities to get into the meaning—or **subtext**—behind the lines without having to keep picking up the script or calling for help with the lines. Having the lines memorized also allows actors to focus more fully on their characters' interactions with other players. But in general, the process of learning the lines happens gradually as a natural part of learning more about the character, the play, and the overall production. Building a character, besides taking time, is based on several interrelated elements: the script, your understanding and interpretation of the character you're playing, your relationship with the other characters, your response to all that happens in the play, and the guidance you receive from the director.

For now, let's focus on the script. In addition to keeping a journal as part of the learning process during rehearsals, actors will also mark up their scripts with notes about the blocking, instructions from the director, and notes to themselves about their character's objectives, motivations, gestures, speech patterns, etc. A highlighter and a supply of pencils are the perfect tools for this kind of note taking. The

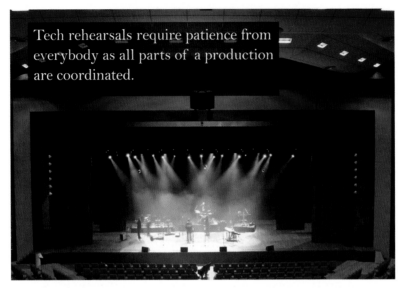

Tech rehearsals require patience from everybody as all parts of a production are coordinated.

first thing I do when I begin working on a script is to highlight all of my lines and any stage directions provided by the playwright. In the course of rehearsals, I'll write in pencil in the margins my notes about the character and instructions from the director. I use a pencil since my interpretation of the character is sure to change as I learn more about him.

I find that it's easier to learn my lines when I have a strong grasp of the plot and of my character's objectives and motivations—in other words, his goals and the reasons he's pursuing them. Some actors learn their lines before blocking begins. Not me. Once I experience moving as my character, I begin to feel the words in the muscles of my body, and this physical connection speeds up the process of memorization. Of course, there comes a time in every actor's life when he or she has to start learning the lines by heart. One way to do this is to record every scene you're in on a tape recorder. This means recording your lines and the lines of all the characters who are also in the scene.

Now, start working on one scene at a time. Play it back several times, listening very carefully to the dialogue while picturing what happens as vividly as you can. When you feel ready, try saying your lines out loud as you listen to the playback. If you forget some of them, just go back to the script and reread the lines you've forgotten. Then press rewind and try saying them without the script. Repeat this process for each scene.

Another method for memorizing your lines is to go through the script, one scene at a time, but without the use of a tape recorder. Read a line or two out loud several times. Then cover the page and try saying them from memory. Forget something? No problem. Uncover the page, read the lines you've forgotten several more times, and try again to say them from memory. Go through the entire scene this way until you feel ready to move on to the next scene.

But wait a minute! We're forgetting something: you also have to know your **cue** lines. These are the lines spoken by another character just before it's your turn to speak. So memorize both your lines and your cue lines. A great way to do this is to rehearse with a partner. She can deliver the cue lines as many times as you need for you to learn when it's your turn at-bat.

Showtime!

Rehearsals have been going along smoothly. The actors are finally off book. The blocking is complete. The characters are coming to life, becoming three-dimensional creations. Each scene has its own mood, texture, and atmosphere. The set designers have done a fantastic job. So have the costumers. All the props are in place. The play as a whole is acquiring a definite shape with rising and falling action, and a clear, strong climax. Showtime is just around the corner. But before the excitement of opening night, some finishing touches still need doing—tech and dress rehearsals.

Tech rehearsals are when the sound and lighting crews rehearse their cues with (and without) the actors. In this "cue-to-cue" rehearsal, the people who manage the lighting and sound need to make sure the effects happen when they're supposed to happen and the equipment functions without any glitches. For example, actor A and actor B are on stage. When actor A says, "Why didn't you tell me you wrecked my car?" the lighting person brings up a warm red light. The actor's line is the cue line for the lighting person. Instead of playing out the entire scene, the actors move on to the next lighting cue until all the cues have been rehearsed.

The sound designer, who has created the music and/or sound effects for the play, also needs to run cues with the actors. Sound cues can be done together with lighting cues or separately, depending on their complexity and the preferences of the director.

Once the technical aspects of the show are in place and any glitches in the equipment have been eliminated, it's time for the dress rehearsal. For the dress rehearsal, the actors perform the entire play in costume and makeup, and the technical crew executes all the lighting and sound cues. In a successful dress rehearsal, all the parts will mesh, and the play will be ready to present to an audience. In some productions, a theater may also offer one or more **preview** performances before the play officially opens. Previews allow the director and crew to fix any problems that arose during the dress rehearsals or to make last-minute changes.

After the previews comes opening night—the night the cast and production crew have been preparing for. By now, the publicity has gone out to the press and social media. All the people involved in the play have spread the news about the opening among their own networks of friends and family. At the theater, the lights are on and the doors are open. The audience is beginning to arrive. Some people have already reserved their tickets; others will buy them at the box office inside the theater.

Volunteers hand out programs. Ushers lead eager audience members to their seats. Perhaps the reviewers also arrive. Backstage, the actors are going over their lines one last time, checking their makeup, making any final adjustments to their costumes, warming up their bodies and voices, and checking their props to be certain they're all there and accessible.

Meanwhile, the stage manager is overseeing the pre-performance preparation. Using a headset or intercom, the stage manager is in touch with the staff in the front of the house. He wants to make sure the lobby is clear and the theater's front doors are closed. The answer comes back: yes. Now he gives the technical crew a warning cue. They have one minute to get everything ready. The minute passes. The stage manager cues the cast and the crew to stand by. Seconds to go. The stage manager calls "**places**." The actors move to their assigned spots to start the play.

House lights dim. The audience quiets. Stage lights come up. The stage manager gives one more cue: go! The magic begins with the opening scene

During the performance, actors who are not on stage can relax in the "green room," a waiting area or lounge for the performers and members of the production staff. Although there are a number of possible explanations for the term "green room," some historians think the term comes from a time when such rooms were painted green.

Actors might also head to the dressing room to change costumes, fix their makeup, or go over their lines with another actor or on their own. A verbal cue from the stage manager or a lighting cue in the green room will signal actors that a new scene is beginning and they need to get ready to go on stage.

Curtain Call

When the show is over, the actors return to the stage for what is called a **curtain call**, to take a bow and receive the applause of the audience. Typically, the supporting players return first, followed by the **principals** in the order of their relative importance. The leading actors are the last to appear.

The actors may have to bow several times if an enthusiastic audience keeps clapping in response to their performance. When they finish their bowing, the actors will gesture toward the technical staff to acknowledge their support and to cue the audience to clap for them as well.

On opening night, after the performance, bouquets of flowers, flung from appreciative members of the

The curtain call gives every member of the cast, from the least to the leads, a chance to bask in applause.

audience, are apt to be strewn on the stage—a sure sign that the show has been well received. Once the audience has left the theater, stagehands can begin putting away props and cleaning up the house, or auditorium, and the stage. Backstage, the actors will be busy removing their makeup and changing out of their costumes and into their street clothes.

In keeping with an old tradition, the last person to leave the theater switches on the "ghost light," a single bulb upstage center, meant to keep away unfriendly spirits and to make sure that when cast and crew return, they won't have to cross a dark stage.

A functioning harness supports Spider-Man as he completes another death-defying leap.

CHAPTER FOUR

MISSTEPS AND HOW TO AVOID THEM

In this chapter, we'll take a look at some of the common missteps beginning actors are likely to take as they grapple with the challenges of playing a role and being onstage. We'll also consider some tried-and-true techniques for avoiding these missteps and staying on course.

Sometimes in theater, a misstep, or mistake, is not the fault of the actor. It could be the result of faulty set design, for example, or the failure of a piece of technical equipment. In December 2010, a Broadway theater mounted a production of *Spider-Man: Turn Off the Dark*. At a crucial moment in the play, Spiderman was supposed to leap off a bridge and perform a daring maneuver to rescue his girlfriend. His stunt double executed the first part—leaping off the bridge. Unfortunately, the safety harness he was wearing flew open, and the poor man plummeted 30 feet (9 meters), crashing into the orchestra pit. He survived and eventually recovered, but the crash landing fractured his skull and broke his ribs. The accident wasn't the stunt double's fault; the fault was with the safety harness, which a crew member may have failed to adjust correctly.

Speaking Too Softly

Fortunately, missteps committed by beginning actors are rarely so dramatic or life threatening. However, they can still take away from the quality of the show. One of the most common missteps is for actors to think that a normal speaking voice is loud enough for a live performance. If you can hear yourself, and your fellow actors can also hear you, then the audience will hear you too. No way! While this may be true in a theater with excellent acoustics, your stage voice needs to be "cranked up" to an appropriate volume, so even people sitting in the last row can plainly hear you.

So how can you make sure your onstage voice is loud enough? One way is to have a friend sit in the last row and record you delivering your lines, using what you think is an adequate volume. Then listen to the recording. Chances are the playback will be proof enough that you need to work on projection, which is sending your voice as far as it needs to travel during a performance without straining your vocal cords.

Another technique for learning how to project your voice is to experience what it feels like to speak at the correct volume. Then practice speaking at that volume until it begins to come more easily and not sound forced. And remember: the audience not only needs to hear you; they need to understand what you're saying. Reciting tongue twisters and practicing various vocal exercises will improve your ability to clearly articulate your lines.

Turning Away from the Audience

In general, it's never a good idea for actors to turn away from the audience, especially when delivering their lines. It's almost impossible for the audience to hear what the actors are saying when they've got their backs turned. A helpful rule of thumb is for actors to practice the three-quarters rule. Even if your character is not speaking or moving in a particular scene, and your head is facing upstage (away from the audience), make sure three-quarters of your body is viewable by the audience. The main thing is to stay connected with your audience. You want to keep them engaged with you as the character instead of seeing you as a motionless body taking up space on the stage.

Wearing the Cloak of Invisibility

Some inexperienced actors may assume that if they're onstage but not saying anything, then the audience can't see them, or at least is not paying any attention to them. And if that's the case, then they can break character and talk with a fellow actor, or stand there looking bored. The same holds true for actors who are backstage, in the wings or some other part of the theater. If they can't see the audience, then the audience can't see (or hear) them, so they're free to gab, joke around, or whatever.

To avoid the mistake of believing they're "invisible," actors need to bear a few things in mind: If they can see the audience, then the audience will probably be able to see them. If they break character while onstage or fool around backstage, they will distract the audience from paying attention to the main action of the play, and that will hurt the production, something you don't want to do if you consider yourself a team player.

These two actors have broken character as they are unable to contain their laughter.

Breaking Character

Have you ever watched a **blooper** reel? This is a sequence of mistakes made by the actors during the filming of a movie or TV show. The bloopers typically show the actors breaking character in the middle of a scene. To break character means to destroy the illusion that you *are* the part you're

THE AUTHOR'S BIG BLOOPER

It all began with a tough bag of potato chips. As soon as I clamped my teeth on that tightly sealed bag and tried to rip it open, I felt a stabbing pain in my front tooth. That's when I knew I'd have to see the dentist.

A root canal when I was fourteen had killed this tooth. Eventually, the crown had become so brittle that too much pressure would cause it to break. Fast-forward a few weeks after my encounter with the potato chips. I'm performing in a play for middle-school audiences. My dentist had given me a temporary crown, which he had glued to the root. Just in case the crown came loose, I kept a tube of commercial dental adhesive with me at all times.

The character I'm playing is the legendary lumberjack Paul Bunyan. Unexpectedly, the glue loses its grip, and my front tooth sails out of my mouth and lands on the far side of the stage. But I don't break character. Instead, I curl my upper lip over my front teeth to hide the gap and make Paul sound like an old, toothless prospector searching for something onstage. Luckily, I soon find the missing tooth. While my scene partner continues the scene, I duck behind the curtain, squeeze a blob of adhesive on to the root, and then jam the tooth into the adhesive. Presto! I'm young Paul Bunyan once more, ready to bounce back into the show.

playing instead of the person you are in everyday life. As long as an actor is onstage, he or she must remain in character. One way in which inexperienced actors break character during a performance is to respond, as themselves, to something the other actors are saying or doing, If the dialogue or the actions are especially humorous, actors may be tempted to break out laughing instead of remaining in character.

Exits and entrances are perfect opportunities for actors to make a major misstep: entering a scene out of character or dropping their character the minute they exit. The life of the part you're playing doesn't end when a scene is over and you leave the stage. As part of your acting preparation, you need to know your character's **through line**—what is going on in his life between the scenes. When you exit, you're re-entering that life, and when you return to the stage, you're coming from whatever was going on in your character's life before your entrance.

Another reason for breaking character is when something goes wrong. Even experienced actors have been known to "go up" during a scene. When actors "go up," they have forgotten their lines and may not have the slightest clue about what comes next in the scene. For a pro, this sudden "blanking" is usually temporary, and the play goes on. But for a beginner, it can feel terrifying. To relieve this anxiety, the actor might grab the first word that comes to mind, which could very well be the word "sorry," which he addresses to the audience as himself. In effect, he's saying, "I'm sorry I forgot my lines. I hope you'll forgive me. I'm new at this. Just give me a moment to get back on track."

The costume for *Mrs. Doubtfire* presents the lead character as a stereotype.

Getting back on track is the right move. Saying sorry, however, is not. To keep their cool and avoid breaking out of character even when they "go up," actors can practice saying their lines in the wrong sequence and then finding their way back while remaining in character. During the performance, if you lose your way, keep talking. The audience won't know if you're saying the correct lines or not. They only know what they're seeing and hearing. So give them something to hear and see until the right words jump back into your head.

Relying on Stereotypes

A young person playing the part of an older person, such as a grandmother, might color her hair gray, put on a "granny dress," and hobble around onstage with a bad case of the shakes. This actor is playing a stereotype—a conventional, mostly unrealistic image of her character. Instead of working hard to develop a believable character with a unique personality, she's opted for the easy way out.

So how do you avoid relying on stereotypes when you're developing a role? One way is to look carefully at the people around you. Study their movements, their facial expressions, their ways of speaking and dressing. If you're playing an older person, focus your observations on people of a certain age. Your aim as an actor is to see through stereotypes and discover what makes your character unique.

To achieve this, create a detailed backstory of your character's life before the action in the play. Write down what your character wants in each scene and what obstacles are in her way. For a character who is much older than you, you could also ask yourself what her fondest memories are. What did she dream of accomplishing in her life when she was your age? What did she love most or hate most in her life? Questions like these will help you transform your character into a specific, believable individual.

Ignoring the Director's Notes

During rehearsals and performances, the director is observing the action onstage and is taking notes. Part of his or her job is to enable the actors to improve their performance through every stage of the production process, right up to opening night and beyond. Actors who disregard these notes or don't take them seriously are doing a disservice to themselves and to the play.

Not paying attention to the director's notes can harm your performance and the play.

If you disagree with a note, the best course of action is to talk it over with your director. Politely explain why you believe your character wouldn't do what the note is telling him to do. It's possible the director will see your point of view and not have a problem with your disregarding the note.

A Nasty Case of Stage Fright

It's not unusual for first-time actors as well as seasoned pros to experience stage fright—that overwhelming, heart-thumping, cold and clammy, butterflies-in-the-stomach feeling that you just can't go out there and face an audience. Your confidence is shattered. The fear of making a complete fool of yourself has taken over your entire emotional life, and there's nothing you can do to escape this fear and get on with the show.

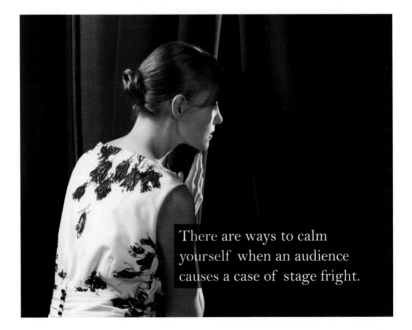

There are ways to calm yourself when an audience causes a case of stage fright.

Stage fright is a scary thing. Instead of releasing your creativity, it can freeze you up inside and keep you from performing at your best. If you should ever find yourself standing in the wings or sitting in the dressing room with a nasty case of stage fright, remind yourself that you deserve to be where you are—ready to go onstage. You got the part after an audition, you worked hard during rehearsals, you followed directions, and you've succeeded in capturing the heart and soul of your character. Now it's time to share your work with an audience.

And don't forget to breathe. Use your breath to relax. Try this: inhale slowly to a count of four, then exhale slowly to a count of four. Repeat this sequence until you begin to feel the tension ebbing. Remember: You're not alone. You're part of a team with your fellow actors. Depend on them. They've got your back, and chances are they're feeling as shaky and unsure as you. So be brave, and act your socks off.

Good Manners for Actors

It's probably fair to say that every occupation has its own set of rules for how to behave. Acting in theater is no different. These rules are a kind of etiquette—guidelines for knowing what is and isn't acceptable. They apply to your interactions with fellow actors and your behavior onstage as well as offstage:

1. Wear comfortable, loose-fitting clothes to rehearsals; since you'll be making notes, be

sure to bring something to write with and on. A notebook and pencil will suffice.

2. Be on time for rehearsals. If the call time for a rehearsal is 7:00 p.m., arrive at the theater by at least 6:30 so you have time to warm up, review any notes from the previous rehearsal, and start the new rehearsal fully present and ready to work.

3. Listen to what the director tells you; take the director's notes seriously and incorporate them into your work.

4. Never give an acting note to another actor. Also, never accept an acting note from anyone but the director. If you have an issue with something a fellow actor is doing during a scene, discuss this with the director, not the actor. Similarly, never tell members of the technical crew how to do their job.

5. If you need to practice using your props, arrange with the director or stage manager to come to the theater between rehearsals. Before every rehearsal and performance, check your props to make sure they're where they're supposed to be and ready for you to use. When you're done using them, return them to their proper place. If any of them are missing or damaged, be sure to notify the stage manager.

6. Once you have received your particular costume or set of costumes, do not alter them in any way. If something feels uncomfortable,

bring this to the attention of the director or costumer.

7. Keep the green room and the dressing room clean and tidy. Avoid bringing any food or beverage into the dressing room where an accidental spill can damage or ruin costumes and/or makeup supplies.

8. Be sure to follow the action of the play so you don't miss the cue for your next entrance. Whatever you do, don't watch the play from the wings; during a performance, this area needs to be kept clear, so actors can easily get on and off stage, and crew members can perform their duties.

9. When you're offstage, talk softly to avoid disturbing or distracting the actors who are performing onstage.

10. While waiting in the wings to enter the stage for your next scene, be sure you can't see the audience. If you can see them, then they can see you, and that's something you don't want until you're onstage and in the scene.

Experiece performing on stage can put you at ease when doing a presentation.

CHAPTER FIVE

APPLYING ACTING EXPERIENCE

Are you thinking about pursuing a career in acting? Do you sometimes fantasize about making it into the big time with your name in lights and adoring fans waiting in line for your autograph? If you're in high school, you might be considering majoring in theater arts in college to prepare you for an acting career. According to the journal *U.S. News & World Report* in 2012, "The riches and glamour of movie stars is not the reality of most college graduates with a drama and theater arts degree. Recent graduates can expect an average salary of $26,000 and an unemployment rate of 7.8 percent. With experience, however, majors can boost their salary to $45,000."

That's not very encouraging news, especially since the cost of living keeps going up, and many graduates are saddled with a huge bill for their college education. Even so, each year thousands of young people aspire to become actors and are willing to make the necessary sacrifices to make their dreams a reality. This could mean accepting a nonprofessional job like waiting tables or doing temporary office work while auditioning for roles in plays, movies, commercials, or other types of media that employ actors. The sense of personal fulfillment that comes from following a career in the creative arts—whether acting, dancing, writing, or some other endeavor— can bring a deep sense of personal fulfillment that outweighs the risks and drawbacks.

But there's more to the story: Even if you don't want to become a professional actor, for whatever reason, the experience of working in the theater can give you a range of marketable skills. Marketable means you can transfer these skills to jobs in other fields that offer both financial and personal rewards. So let's look at some of these skills and occupations in which you could apply them.

Effective Communication

Salespeople, real estate agents, teachers, instructors and trainers, therapists, administrators, managers— these are a sample of the many career options in which effective communication skills are essential. Acting is all about communication, with the audience and with other performers. To perform her part well, an actor needs to develop her ability to speak clearly, with good diction, and to convey her character's emotions and purposes. An effective performance succeeds in connecting with the audience, so the people sitting out there in the darkened auditorium feel what the character is feeling and experience what she is going through in the course of the play.

An actor also learns how to memorize lines. This skill comes in very handy when preparing a sales pitch, getting ready to make a presentation in a meeting, or even when managing people.

Marketing, public relations, and advertising have changed dramatically with the reach of the internet. There are many more outlets for content than there were in the early 2000s. This content must be written, filmed, edited, coordinated, and in some cases, dramatized, all skills that can be learned while working on a theater production. Businesses must learn to tell their story; someone who has done some acting can help them do that.

Creative Problem Solving

Practically every occupation requires the ability to correctly identify problems and come up with possible solutions, including those that may not have occurred to anyone else. Albert Einstein, one of the world's greatest scientists, once said the following: "If I had an hour to solve a problem, I'd spend fifty-five minutes thinking about the problem and five minutes thinking about solutions." His approach to most things in life was highly creative. In today's world, we might say he thought "outside of the box." That's what creative people do, and actors are nothing if not creative. They begin rehearsals with only the written words of their characters. And from these words, which a playwright has written, the actor creates a character that he brings to life on stage and in the hearts and minds of an audience.

A common assumption is that what artists do is creative, while people who work in other occupations aren't so lucky. Actually, creativity is a very important skill not only in the arts but in just about every field of human endeavor, including business, education, medicine, sports, and science. Creativity is especially valuable when it comes to solving problems, whether at home or in the workplace.

Creative problem solving involves sidestepping our routine, conventional way of looking at things and coming up with a brand new, maybe even radical solution to a problem. Careers in marketing, communications, advertising, design, and architecture, to name a few, all need creative people; people with acting experience are already one step ahead of the game when it comes to exercising creativity.

Theater prepares you to work on group projects.

LIFE AFTER THEATER

When she was a child, Allison Ford dreamed of becoming an actress. One day she would take Broadway by storm, and her career would zoom upward with no end in sight. For much of her childhood, Allison studied acting and performed in shows. Later on, she majored in theater arts at college and did so well that she was confident her dream was destined to come true.

Like so many other young people with stars in their eyes, Allison moved to New York City, the "place to be" for aspiring actors. She got an agent and began auditioning for both stage and on-camera work in TV and film. Her talent and acting experience enabled her to land roles in a variety of productions. But when she was only twenty-six, Allison decided to give up her lifelong dream and follow a different path—working as a professional writer. As of 2016, she was the senior writer on the digital team for Sephora cosmetics stores.

In her blog, allisonford.com, she reports that her short-lived acting career had a downside that made her wonder if acting was what she really wanted to do for the rest of her life. She attributes her decision to begin a new career to the internet, where she discovered it was possible to earn a living by writing, which she finds far more satisfying than acting. Thanks to her background in theater, she got her first writing job as a theater and film critic and has since become a successful writer and editor of creative nonfiction for women.

Teamwork

Actors are team players. They have to be. There's no room in the theater for actors who are only thinking of themselves. Cast members need to work together, or the show won't go on. Of course, conflicts and disagreements are bound to arise, and actors may occasionally give more attention to their egos than to the success of the play. But overall, putting on a play requires a high degree of teamwork.

And teamwork is very much a part of life in the world outside the theater. In many corporate settings, a top-down, hierarchical model of authority is no longer the norm. The new norm is to organize employees into project teams or management teams. Even a project manager is still part of the team and not an isolated overlord dictating from above.

Putting on a play also requires meeting deadlines. The show must go on. So taking part in theater teaches students to work under pressure and to get things done on time. These are valuable skills in the business world.

At one time, airline pilots were the highest authority in a chain of command. Other members of the flight crew were expected to defer to the pilot's judgment and follow his orders without question. But those days are disappearing like vapor trails in the sky. The new model depends a whole lot more on teamwork. Of course, the pilot (captain) is still in charge and remains responsible for what happens aboard the plane. But now, pilots (who include both men and women) perform their duties as part of a team. As recent scientific studies have shown, the flight crew, including the captain, needs to coordinate their actions and work closely with air traffic controllers and flight dispatchers.

Employers are seeking to hire people who can work well with others. A good team player also assumes his share of responsibility for the work being done. He also contributes ideas and suggestions and is open to constructive criticism. Sound familiar? If you have acting experience, then you've already had an opportunity to develop these very same skills.

Empathy, or Understanding Others

For actors to portray characters effectively, they have to be able to enter that fictional person's field of vision, to see the world through their eyes, and to have empathy for them. If they judge their character harshly or fail to make strong connections with the character's deepest needs, their portrayal will fall short of its mark and leave the audience unmoved. The ability to have empathy for others requires a degree of self-awareness. What this means for an actor is getting in touch with her own needs, feelings, desires, strengths, and weaknesses. Without this awareness, an actor will have a hard time relating to a character who is very different from himself or herself.

The ability to listen to and understand others is a skill. Actors have it (or need to develop it if they don't have it). Other occupations also need people with this skill. Psychologists, teachers, school

Acting experience can help therapists and counselors to listen and react to clients.

guidance counselors, social workers, ministers, and others following religious vocations are among the many occupations for which empathy is a necessary qualification.

Improvisation

According to legend, the eighteenth-century Scottish poet Robert Burns was plowing his field one day when the blade of his plow accidentally destroyed a mouse's nest. With the plow handle still in his hand (or so his brother claimed), Burns composed a poem as an apology to the mouse. A phrase in the poem reads "The best laid schemes o' mice an' men / Gang aft agley." A popular interpretation is "Even the best laid plans of mice and men often go awry." In other words, no matter how well we prepare for something, there's no telling what will happen or what will go wrong.

Bloopers during a play (or other types of live performances) are a great example of things going wrong. No matter how carefully the actors and the production crew have prepared, the unexpected can still take everybody by total surprise. A light cue is missed; part of the stage set collapses; the seat of an actor's pants rips open; the sound effect of a ringing phone goes off at the wrong moment; an actor forgets to enter during his next scene. You get the picture. Onstage, actors have to handle the unexpected, and this means being able to improvise—to come up, on the spot, in the heat of the moment, with a reasonable response to a situation they had no way of foreseeing. That's what it means to improvise.

Improvisation is a skill. When something goes awry on stage, actors who lack this skill are likely to become flustered, not knowing what to do. Here's an example of two actors who didn't let a blooper throw them off their game. Instead, they improvised, much to the audience's delight. During a performance of the Broadway musical comedy *Dirty Rotten Scoundrels,* one of the actors is supposed to shoot John Lithgow (former star of the hit television series *3rd Rock from the Sun*). But she doesn't have the prop gun! Oops!

Improvising, she points her index finger as if it were a gun and "shoots." The audience hears the sound effect of a gunshot. Several seconds pass. Lithgow is still standing instead of falling dead. Then he goes offstage and returns with the missing gun, which he hands to his would-be killer. The audience bursts out laughing. The show continues. This brief improvisation was a smashing success.

In the workplace, with few exceptions, people are sure to encounter the unexpected, and when they do, it will be necessary to improvise. Closely related to the ability to improvise is flexibility, being able to adapt to change. When sudden changes and difficulties occur, a flexible person stays calm (ideally) and comes up with alternative strategies for handling problems. Say you are in a room with other vendors trying to win a contract, and the client changes the requirements for the job. Thinking quickly and coming up with solutions rather than panicking can bring in business. Employers will notice. Working in the theater can help you become more flexible while honing your ability to improvise.

Outside of the theater, you can apply these skills in any number of careers and occupations. Consider athletic coaches. They can never be absolutely sure their game plans will succeed, so they have to be ready to improvise. If a star player is injured on the field, the coach will have to substitute a different player on the spot. Or suppose the opposing team is pulling out all the stops and taking the lead. Whatever strategies had been developed off the field will need to be adapted or abandoned to avoid defeat.

Actor John Lithgow kept his cool when a mistake was made in *Dirty Rotten Scoundrels*.

Improvisation can prepare television journalists for any situation on camera.

Imagine you're working as a television journalist. Maybe you landed the job because working in a community theater had helped you fine-tune your communication and presentation skills. You are reporting live on a standoff between police and a gunman with hostages for a local news program. As you give your prepared update on the situation, gunfire breaks out a good distance behind you. The update is now old news and the cameras are on. You must improvise while simultaneously trying to find out what is going on.

In another scenario, you're a trial lawyer handling a big case. Your actor's training has come in handy: you know how to reach the witnesses, how to get across your client's story as effectively as you once pursued your characters' objectives onstage. But now, in the courtroom, the opposing legal team has filed an objection, and the judge agrees with them. Evidence gets thrown out. With little time to prepare, you need to change your strategy. You can do it, thanks in part to all the times you have improvised your lines during a performance, or dealt with missing props or unanticipated scene changes.

Improvisation doesn't just mean "winging it," although there are occasions when that's exactly what needs to happen. In a larger sense, the ability to improvise involves a willingness to change, to be fully open to new information or new ideas instead of clinging to whatever may have worked in the past. If you can do these things, chances are you'll find a home in the fast-changing environment of the modern workplace.

GLOSSARY

acoustics The quality of sound within a closed space, such as an auditorium.

arc The overall direction of a character's story or journey in a play, movie, or TV show.

articulation The clear pronunciation of words.

backstory A character's past, including the people and circumstances that have contributed to his or her present situation.

blocking The exact staging of the actors' movements onstage.

blooper An unintended, often funny moment during a performance or rehearsal.

cue A line in a play that tells an actor or other person involved in a play that it is time to take action, such as speaking a line.

curtain call The actors' return to the stage at the end of the performance to receive applause and recognition from the audience.

diction A style of pronouncing words when speaking or singing.

ensemble A cohesive group of performers working together toward the shared goal of staging and performing a play or other type of performance.

feminism The movement to guarantee and protect the rights and equal opportunities of women.

headshot A specific type of photograph that shows a person's actual appearance. Actors and models use headshots to represent themselves on social media and for auditions.

monologue A long speech performed by one actor.

objective The goal a character is trying to achieve in a scene. A super-objective is what the character is attempting to achieve in the course of the entire play.

obstacles Whatever prevents a character in a play from achieving his or her objectives.

off book Actors who are off book during rehearsals have learned their lines and only use the script when necessary.

places The locations on or off stage where actors position themselves before the start of a performance.

prima donna A person who can be difficult to work with because of their exaggerated sense of importance. Also, the lead female singer in an opera.

principals The leading performers in a play, film, or TV show.

projection The action of making one's voice audible to an audience while appearing to speak normally.

Restoration The time period that began with the restoration of the exiled Charles II to the English throne in 1660. Restoration comedy, written during this period, typically poked fun at the upper class.

soliloquy A theatrical device in which a character expresses his or her thoughts to an audience when other characters are either not present or not listening.

substitution A method used by actors to find elements from their own lives that are comparable to elements in the lives of the characters they're playing.

subtext The deeper meaning within or between the lines of a play.

through line For an actor, the through line connects their character's objectives from one scene to the next; it explains the character's actions throughout the play.

FOR MORE INFORMATION

Books

Belli, Mary Lou, and Dinah Lenney. *Acting for Young Actors: The Ultimate Teen Guide.* Washington, DC: Back Stage Books, 2006.

Friedman, Lise. *Break a Leg!: The Kids' Guide to Acting & Stagecraft.* New York: Workman Publishing Company, Inc., 2002.

McTigue, Mary. *Acting Like a Pro.* White Hall, VA: Betterway Publications, Inc., 1992.

Milstein, Janet B. *The Ultimate Audition Book for Teens: 111 One-Minute Monologues.* Hanover, NH: Smith & Kraus Publishers Inc., 2000.

Surface, Mary Hall. *Short Scenes and Monologues for Middle School Actors.* Hanover, NH: Smith & Kraus Publishers Inc., 2000.

Websites

American Association of Community Theater
http://www.aact.org
This website for the American Association of Community Theater provides a wide range of resources, including how to run a theater company and how to stage a show.

The Inner Actor
http://theinneractor.com/acting-resources
This valuable website provides online courses, instruction, and links to resources for actors and their parents.

Master Talent Teachers
http://www.mastertalentteachers.com/actors/ confidence-and-becoming-a-great-actor
In a short essay, Master Talent Teachers comment on the importance of achieving confidence as an actor.

Memorize Your Lines
http://www.wikihow.com/Memorize-Your-Lines
Straightforward, illustrated tips for how beginning actors can learn their lines.

StageMilk
http://www.stagemilk.com
This great resource for actors and drama teachers provides essays related to theater. It includes recommended acting games, monologues, vocal warm-ups, articulation exercises, and acting scenes.

Videos

An Acting Masterclass from Michael Caine
https://www.youtube.com/watch?v=-hEpUV4_qeY
Sir Michael Caine provides advice for actors in an interview at the BBC.

Master Talent Teachers
http://www.mastertalentteachers.com/acting-videos
Students can find a wealth of instruction from the Master Talent Teachers video vault.

Robert De Niro—One Minute of Brilliant Acting Advice
https://www.youtube.com/watch?v=S4K2znuYjwI
Hollywood actor Robert De Niro gives very useful, practical acting advice in one minute!

INDEX

Page numbers in **boldface** are illustrations. Entries in **boldface** are glossary terms.

ABOUT THE AUTHOR

George Capaccio is an actor as well as a professional writer. His introduction to acting in theater came about as a result of his wife's work in a community theater production. When a fellow actor dropped out of the cast, she asked George if he would step into the role. He did—at the age of twenty-eight. It was his first acting experience and, for George, the beginning of a new career in theater.